MYSTERY!!
MYSTERY!!
MYSTERY!!

Mysterious Places

Katie Dicker

A+
Smart Apple Media

Published by Smart Apple Media,
an imprint of Black Rabbit Books
P.O. Box 3263, Mankato, Minnesota, 56002
www.blackrabbitbooks.com

Designed by Hel James
Edited by Mary-Jane Wilkins

Cataloging-in-Publication Data is available from the Library of Congress

ISBN 978-1-62588-204-2

Photo acknowledgements
title page Brandelet/Shutterstock; pages 2-3 Gelia/Thinkstock;
5 Zoran Karapancev/Shutterstock; 6-7 Linda Bucklin/Thinkstock;
8 WitR; 9 Santia, b somchaij; 10-11 kritskaya; 12 Viktorus;
13 chasethestorm.com; 14-15b Justin Black; 15 Kiev.Victor/all
Shutterstock; 16-17 Roman Sigaev/Thinkstock; 20 Zack Frank/
Shutterstock; 21 NodalPoint/Thinkstock; 22 imageZebra;
24 Brandelet/both Shutterstock
Cover longtaildog/Shutterstock

Artwork Q2A Media Art Bank

Printed in China

DAD0054
032014
9 8 7 6 5 4 3 2 1

Contents

World of Mystery

The world is full of mysterious places. Groups of people, or whole cities, have disappeared. In some places, there are mysteries that still have not been solved...

Special Powers

*Many **sacred sites** in Europe lie on straight lines that cross each other. These are called **ley lines**. Some people think ley lines may have special powers. Perhaps years ago, people used them to channel a mysterious energy.*

Ley lines link many sacred sites in the UK.

4

Time Travel

*In 1901, two teachers from Oxford University, the United Kingdom, were visiting the Palace of Versailles near Paris, France. During their visit, they got lost. As they were trying to find their way, they saw scenes they believed were from 1789— the year of the **French Revolution**. They saw the queen, Marie Antoinette, and they crossed an old bridge that was there in 1789. Did the women somehow slip through time on their trip?*

Does the ghost of Marie Antoinette haunt the Palace of Versailles?

Drowned Cities

All over the world, lost towns and cities lie hidden beneath the sea. Some cities lie so deep that only divers can find them. You can see others at low **tide**.

Rising Water

The first cities recorded were built about 5,000 years ago, but some ruins found under the sea are much older than that. How did these cities become flooded? Some people think that about 10,000 years ago, the last **Ice Age** made the oceans rise and swallow up cities by the sea.

City of Secrets

About 2,000 years ago, there was a busy city called Nan Madol on the island of Pohnpei in the Pacific Ocean. Today, it lies beneath the ocean. Divers have found long stones, and human skeletons more than 6.5 feet (2m) tall! No one knows how these ancient people moved such heavy stones, or what happened to the city.

It's a Mystery!

Nearly 2,500 years ago, a Greek writer called Plato told the story of the lost city of Atlantis. He said the city had been destroyed by fire, and the ruins were beneath the sea. Many people have searched for Atlantis, but no trace of the city has been found.

Desert Secrets

*More than 7,000 years ago, the ancient Egyptians built pyramids as tombs for the **pharaohs**. Their positions seem to line up with the stars. These giant stone structures conceal secrets waiting to be uncovered.*

Strange Discovery

*The Egyptian pyramids are near the Nile River. In 1983, researcher Robert Bauval noticed that the pyramids were in the same formation as Orion, a **constellation** of stars. Two more pyramids would complete the pattern. Perhaps they lie buried beneath the desert sand?*

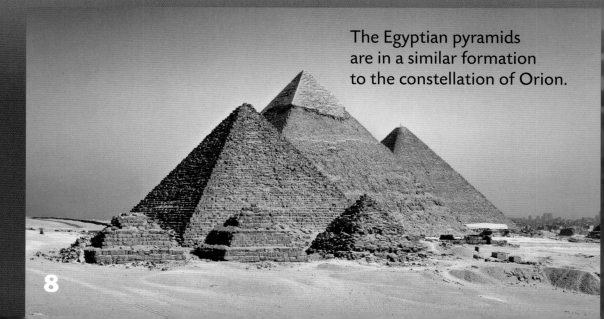

The Egyptian pyramids are in a similar formation to the constellation of Orion.

Mirroring the Stars

Buildings on other ancient sites line up with the stars. A temple called Angkor Thom in Cambodia matches the positions of the stars in the constellation Draco (the dragon). Scientists think that our **ancestors** copied the stars to bring harmony between the Earth and the sky.

The design of Angkor Thom also follows the patterns of the stars.

Mystery Pyramid

Some Egyptian pyramids hide mysterious secrets. The Cheops pyramid has an empty coffin inside. No one knows what happened to the body of the pharaoh Cheops. The pyramid also contains four strange tunnels. One is only 8 inches (20 cm) wide, and blocked by a slab of stone. No one knows what lies behind it...

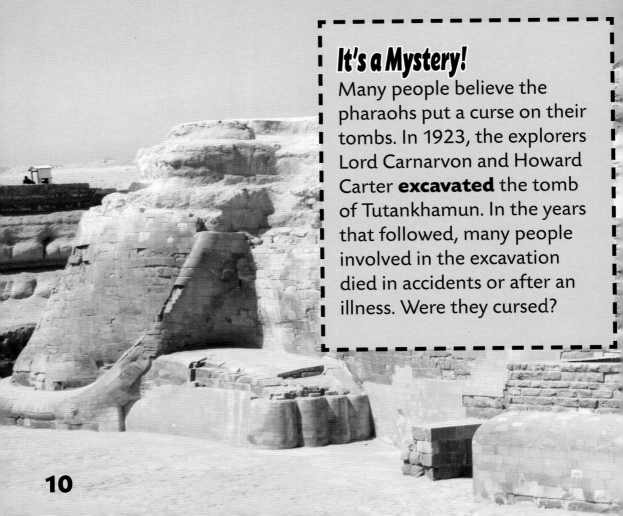

It's a Mystery!

Many people believe the pharaohs put a curse on their tombs. In 1923, the explorers Lord Carnarvon and Howard Carter **excavated** the tomb of Tutankhamun. In the years that followed, many people involved in the excavation died in accidents or after an illness. Were they cursed?

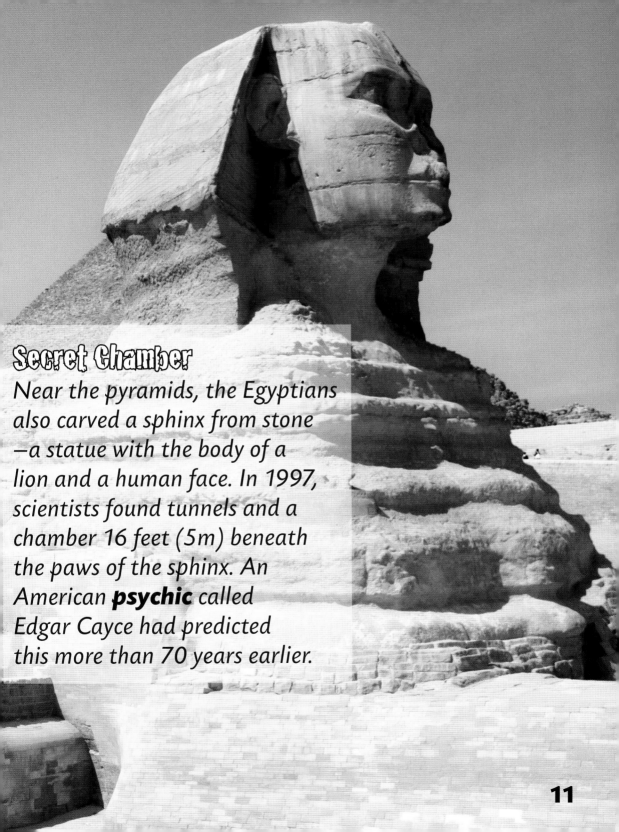

Secret Chamber

Near the pyramids, the Egyptians also carved a sphinx from stone —a statue with the body of a lion and a human face. In 1997, scientists found tunnels and a chamber 16 feet (5m) beneath the paws of the sphinx. An American **psychic** called Edgar Cayce had predicted this more than 70 years earlier.

Giant Structures

Thousands of years ago, ancient sites were built on a grand scale. No one knows exactly how they were made using simple tools.

Pacific Island

On Easter Island in the Pacific Ocean, nearly 900 giant stone statues look out to sea. Scientists believe the 33 feet (10m) tall statues are about 800 years old. The islanders made rollers from tree trunks to move the stones. When all the trees had been cut down, hunting and farming became difficult. Food started to run out and people began to kill and eat each other.

Sky View

In Nazca, Peru, the desert is decorated with huge patterns and pictures of animals and birds. Scientists believe the shapes may have been made when stones were taken from the ground to reveal dusty soil underneath. The shapes can only be seen from the air, but were made long before planes! Did the Nazca people make pictures their gods could see from the sky?

It's a Mystery!

The city of Puma Punku in Bolivia seems to have been destroyed by an earthquake. Only huge pieces of stone remain. The blocks came from a quarry eight miles (16 km) away. They would have been impossible to move when the city was built 2,500 years ago. How did the ancient people of Puma Punku build their city?

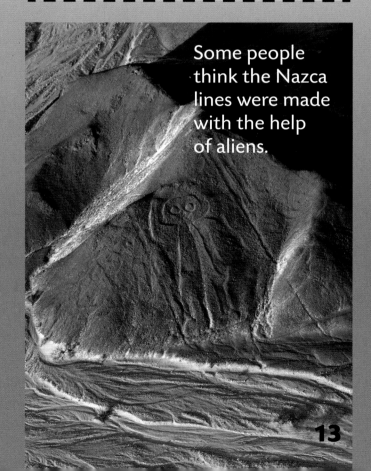

Some people think the Nazca lines were made with the help of aliens.

Secret Circle

In Wiltshire, UK, another giant structure holds many secrets. Stonehenge is a huge ring of standing stones, with horizontal stones balanced on top. Built more than 4,000 years ago, it is about 100 feet (30m) in diameter, and nearly 16 feet (5m) high. **Burial mounds** surround the area, and burnt human remains have been found nearby. No one really knows what Stonehenge was for—perhaps it was a place of healing, or sun worship, or a site of religious **rituals** and **sacrifices**.

Will we ever uncover the secrets of Stonehenge?

Giant Stones

Some of the stones at Stonehenge weigh about 49 tons (45,000 kg). They would have been very difficult to cut and move with simple tools. Scientists think they might have come from a quarry about 25 miles (40 km) away. How did these ancient people carry these mighty stones, and build such an impressive structure?

The giant stones are more than twice the size of a man, so how did these ancient people move them?

Miracle Workers

Sometimes, strange things happen that scientists can't explain. Religious people call these events miracles—the work of gods or saints. No one knows exactly how they happen.

Healing Water

In 1858, Bernadette Soubirous had a strange vision near Lourdes, France. She saw a mysterious woman who told her to drink water from a nearby spring. Afterwards, Bernadette was cured of her asthma. The Catholic Church believes she saw the Virgin Mary—the mother of Jesus. Now, many sick people visit Lourdes each year, hoping to cure their illness.

It's a Mystery!

When Bernadette died, her body didn't **decay**. It is kept in a glass-topped coffin. Although she died nearly 140 years ago, Bernadette's body is still intact. The Catholic Church says this is a miracle.

Life-like Statue

In September 1995, people witnessed a miracle in a temple in New Delhi, India. A statue of the Hindu god Lord Ganesha began to drink milk from a spoon. Soon, statues of gods all over northern India seemed to be drinking milk, too. People rushed out to buy milk so they could offer it to statues of Lord Ganesha themselves.

Did a statue of Lord Ganesha perform a miracle, or is there another explanation?

The Money Pit

In 1795, Daniel McGinnis was hunting on Oak Island off the coast of Canada when he found a strange pit, which remained a mystery for more than 200 years.

Digging Deep

Daniel decided to dig for treasure, but after digging 26 feet (8m), he was tired and gave up. People began to think the pit held pirate treasure. They called it the "Money Pit." Many have tried to reach the bottom, but none has succeeded. In 1971, a video camera lowered into the shaft showed blurred pictures of what appeared to be wooden chests and a human hand!

Natural Barriers

Even with modern drilling equipment, the Money Pit has been difficult to dig. Every 10 feet (3m), a barrier of wood, clay, or stone crosses the shaft. The pit also becomes flooded at high tide. Stones arranged in the shape of a cross have been found nearby. Some people think the pit might hide the Holy Grail —the cup used by Jesus at his last supper.

Many people have tried to dig for treasure in the Money Pit.

The pit's barriers, deep underground, make it difficult to explore.

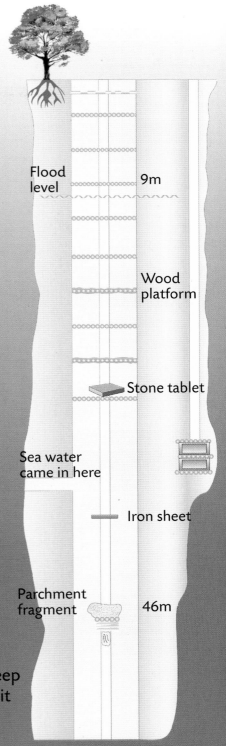

Flood level

9m

Wood platform

Stone tablet

Sea water came in here

Iron sheet

Parchment fragment

46m

Surviving Secrets

Some places hide secrets that have never been uncovered. In parts of the world, groups of people have mysteriously disappeared: no one knows what happened to them.

In 1587, English explorer Walter Raleigh helped to set up the first British **colony** in North America at Roanoke Island, North Carolina. He left 100 people there when he sailed back to England. Three years later, he returned, but the residents had vanished and were never found. Years later, some native American groups in the area had pale skin and blue eyes. Perhaps they were related to the lost colonists?

Fort Raleigh marks the site of America's first British colony—but what happened to the settlers?

Buried Emperor

Qin Shi Huang, the first emperor of China, built a large burial mound to hold his body. Inside was a copy of his empire, with small palaces and flowing rivers. The tomb is said to contain traps which will kill anyone who tries to break in. Many of the builders died while it was being built, or were killed to keep the tomb's secret. No one knows how Qin Shi Huang died and the tomb has never been explored.

An army of life-size pottery soldiers guards the body of Qin Shi Huang.

Glossary

ancestors
Relatives that lived before you.

burial mounds
Heaps of earth that cover buried ancient tombs.

colony
A group of people from one country living in another.

constellation
A group of stars that form a particular pattern.

decay
When something rots and breaks down, it decays.

excavate
To explore or remove by digging.

French Revolution
An uprising in the 1700s, when the people of France turned against their king.

Ice Age
A time when glaciers covered much of the Earth.

ley lines
Imaginary lines linking three or more ancient sites.

pharaohs
Rulers in ancient Egypt.

psychic
A person who is said to read minds, talk to dead people, or predict the future.

rituals
Ceremonies or actions performed in a certain way.

sacred sites
Special places where someone, or something, is worshipped.

sacrifices
Giving something or killing someone as an offering to a god.

tide
The rise and fall of seawater as it moves from its highest level to its lowest, and back again.

Web Sites

www.scaryforkids.com/haunted-stories
True stories of haunted houses and other scary places.

www.mysteriousplaces.com
A closer look at mysterious places, such as Easter Island and Stonehenge.

Index